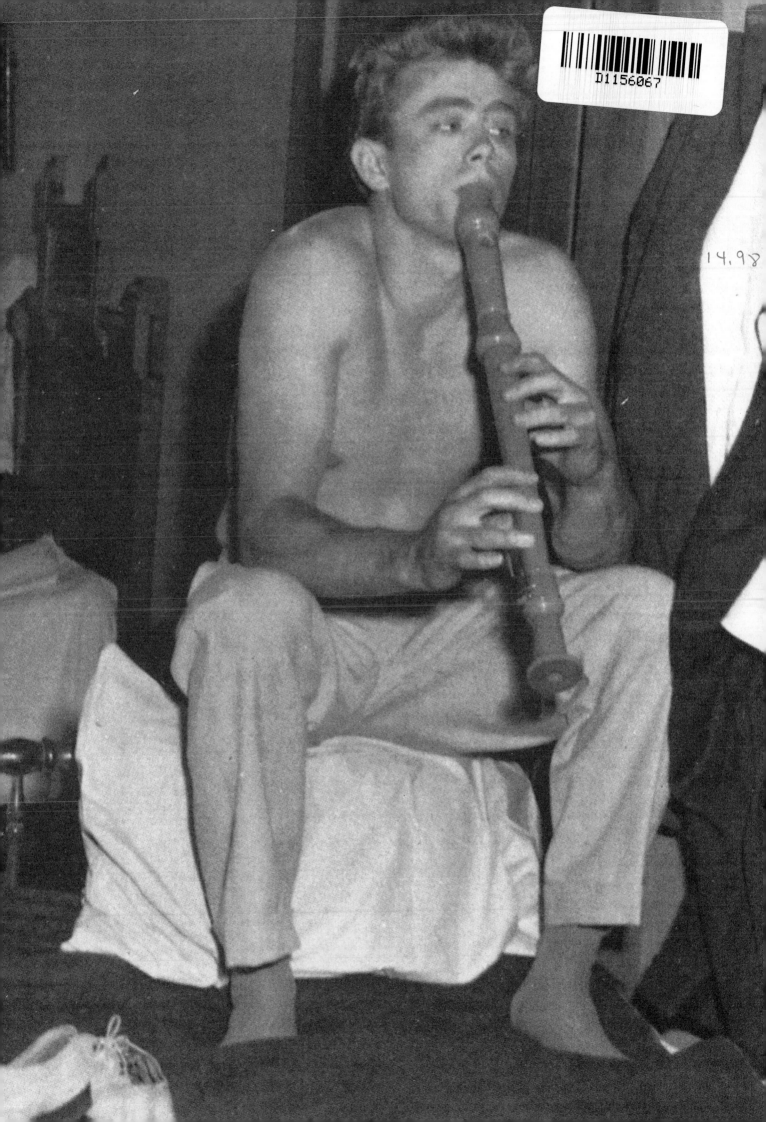

JAMES DEAN. Footsteps of a Giant

Wolfgang J. Fuchs

JAMES DEAN

Footsteps of a Giant

© 1989 Taco Verlagsgesellschaft und Agentur mbH,
Hauptstr. 9, D-1000 Berlin 62
Cover: Peter Feierabend, Berlin
English translation: Hugh Beyer
Cover and Frontispiece: © The John Kobal Collection
ISBN: 3-89268-096-5
Printed in Germany

CONTENTS

PREFACE

James Dean lives! And he works for Barclay's Bank in Swindon! This rather peculiar press bulletin hit the headlines in the seventies. A customer claimed she had recognized him by his windproof jacket and the way he was cleaning his fingernails with a stiletto. At first she thought she had seen a ghost, and when she went back to look at his name plate, the man who seemed to be James Dean put on a pair of sun glasses, turned his back towards her and began to immerse himself in some paper work. The woman was so amazed at what she had seen that she decided to go to a popular London magazine where she was told that there had indeed been a rumour for some time: many people believed that the first teenage idol in the world had not died in a car accident, but disappeared and started a new life under a different name to avoid the inland revenue.

Although this story seems rather far-fetched at first sight, there is neverthe-less a grain of truth in it. James Dean did of course die in a car accident at the age of 24, but he has, in a sense, survived or even transcended his death

James Dean at the time of "Rebel Without a Cause".

by imprinting his screen image onto the hearts and minds of the people who used to watch his films. Both in his films and in his life he embodied a certain feeling of unrest which prevailed among young people in the 1950s. He became an idol and his presence aroused that mass hysteria among his fans which could not be explained by charisma alone. And so he takes his place among a whole series of popular idols who died at an early age and who were said to have faked their deaths.

It is quite extraordinary that an actor who played in such a small number of films should be remembered by so many people, expecially by youngsters, and that he should have been so influential in shaping our ideas of the 1950s. James Dean has become the symbol of a whole lifestyle – the lifestyle of teenagers of the fifties. And his life as an actor was short and extremely intense. His pictures are still with us – like an echo from times gone by, but also an idol for generations to come, thus continuing the James Dean cult beyond his death. So let us put on our jeans, boots and denim jackets and trace the footsteps of a very short life – the footsteps of a giant.

James Dean
Films as a Life – Life as a Film

James Dean was only 24 when – perhaps at the height of his career – he lost his life in a car accident with his Porsche Spyder. His early death may have been partly responsible for his undying fame. But as with most ordinary mortals, the beginning of his life was quite normal.

James Dean was born in Marion, a small industrial town 30 miles north of Indianapolis, on 8 February 1931. We do not know whether this is why he took an interest in racing as a sport. His mother, Mildred Dean, née Wilson, gave him the name James Byron Dean. The first name was that of the doctor who came to the Green Gables Apartments in East Fourth Street and helped with the birth, the middle name was deliberately chosen in honour of her favourite poet, Lord Byron.

James Dean as Cal Trask in "East of Eden".

Pages 8/9: Just as James Dean had to work extremely hard in "Giant", he also had to do so in real life, as an actor.

Names need not always be significant, of course. Nevertheless it is worth noting that Lord Byron, together with his contemporaries Wordsworth and Coleridge, was a rebel against the poetic conventions of the eighteenth century. And in fact he went even further than the other two. He and his followers felt rebellious towards the whole of English society, the Church of England and even the Crown. Byron was a typical rebel of his time. He was only 36 when he died in 1824. James Dean did not become a poet, but he was also the prototype of a rebel and, like Byron, died at a very early age.

When James Dean's mother chose his middle name, she was certainly not thinking of Byron's rebellious nature, but rather the artistic side of his character. The name was to become that of a whole programme for her son – not in any manipulative sense, like the programme of a computer-operated robot, but symbolically. Although Mildred had been brought up on a farm, she always felt very much attracted by the imaginary world of poetry and music.

11

Her husband Winton Dean was a dental technician in the service of the federal government, thus providing a regular income and opening up opportunities for her son which she had been unable to enjoy herself. This story of James Dean's middle name almost sounds too beautiful to be true. But it fits very nicely into the general cult that has been building up around him. The thought that he may have been called Byron after a friend of the Deans' seems rather too banal by comparison. After all, his mother did indeed have a certain artistic talent.

When little Jimmy was still very young, she taught him to play-act, and she also sent him to violin lessons. In fact, she created a whole new world around herself and her son, a world in which James's father hardly played any role at all. Mildred had to put up with a lot of criticism from her relatives who said that she was spoiling the boy. And there may be some truth in it, because when James was a little older and went to school, he felt from the very beginning that there was a certain distance between himself and the other children. To make matters worse, Winton Dean was transferred to Los Angeles when Jimmy was only four years old. This move made it even more difficult for him to relate to other people, and he became more and more dependent on his mother. But the idyllic little world in which they lived was soon to be disrupted by a real disaster: Mildred Dean developed terminal cancer and died when her son was only nine.

His mother's death did not, however, create any kind of bond between him and his father. On the contrary. The gulf between the two became virtually unbridgeable. In the end the disturbed relationship between father and son was so conspicuous that Winton Dean's mother noticed it. And when the Wilsons decided to have Mildred buried in Indiana, old Mrs Dean suggested that they should take not only Mildred's body but also her son back to Indiana. So James Dean returned to his original home and spent the next few years on the farm which belonged to his uncle Marcus and aunt Ortense Winslow in Fairmount, a village not far from Marion. He soon developed a fascination for the Winslows' tractor, which opened up a whole new world to the little boy, the world of machines.

James Dean with his cousin on his uncle's farm in Fairmount.

James Dean as a member of the Fairmount High School baseball team. Here with glasses, which he needed from early childhood onwards.

James's life could have taken a more normal course now, if the Winslows had not had a second child after their daughter Jane. Although James had already started to call the Winslows Mum and Dad, he rather felt that the arrival of their son was something of an instrusion and that it made it even more difficult for him to build up relationship with the people around him. And so he became more and more introverted again. When James had his first motorbike, it was of all people the local vicar, the Rev. James De Weerd, who encouraged him in his enthusiasm for racing. Together with acting, this was to become one of his passions.

As a schoolboy Dean turned out to the brightest child in his class and, in spite of his bad short-sightedness, one of the best at sport. He was also excellent at art and made a name for himself as president of the school drama club. On the other hand, he was prone to sudden violent fits of anger and would lose his temper when he was annoyed.

14

It was at school performances and poetry recital competitions that Dean experienced success for the first time in his life. He also managed to win a sports medal and an art prize. By the time he graduated from Fairmount High School at the age of 18, in 1949, his teachers thought that he was extraordinarily gifted but that he lacked all ambition. But what does that really mean? They simply failed to realize that James Dean's talents were linked to ambition which could not find fulfilment in a rural environment. James Dean was in fact very ambitious. This can be seen in the enthusiasm with which he took up his father's suggestion that he should go to college in California and study for a degree.

However, his father had certain definite ideas as to what would be best for him. He felt that drama was not really a proper academic discipline and that the boy should study law and sport at Santa Monica College. Dean submitted to his father's wishes at first, but soon realized that this was not really his cup of tea. So he transferred to the University College of Los Angeles (UCLA), earning his keep with part-time jobs. One day, during one of his vacations, he went to the cinema in Marion and saw Marlon Brando's debut in Fred Zinnemann's film The Men. The acting impressed him so much that he decided to become a great actor himself.

Then, shortly after the beginning of term, Dean was given a role in a student production of Macbeth. His performance was of such a high standard that he was congratulated by Isabel Draesmer, whose job it was to find talent actors. This was in fact Dean's first step on the road to success – and away from the academic world. At the time he was sharing a bedsitter in Santa Monica with Bill Bast, a fellow-student who later wrote a famous biography of Dean. To pay their rent, the two youngsters took on all sorts of odd jobs in Los Angeles, that city of illusions. Eventually they also came into contact with the radio, television and cinema. When he was filming for a two-minute Pepsi Cola commercial, he was discovered by some agents and offered the role of John the Evangelist in an Austrian television play. And when he was completely ignored by the UCLA dramatic society and not included in the cast for their next play, he finally came to the conclusion that an academic career was not the right thing after all. His next step was to join an actor's study group under the tutorship of William Whitmore, where he learned about the Stanislavski method. The aim was to experience one's own self by following Brando's example and identifying

A Warner Bros. photograph of James Dean, taken specially for the press in 1955.

16

totally with one's role. The emotional difficulties that are involved in this, expecially after the acting is actually over, turned out to be rather problematic for Dean.

Dean and Bill Bast parted company after a quarrel over a girl-friend. Dean was now left on his own and played several minor roles in the films Fixed Bayonets, Sailor Beware and Has Anybody Seen My Gal? and also a number of radio plays. People soon advised Dean not to waste his time on rubbishy little roles in Hollywood and said he should go to New York instead, where he could develop his talent much better. Dean hesitated at first, but one day he suddenly changed his mind and decided to move to the East coast.

With a letter of recommendation in his hand, he went round all the television studios and eventually ended up with a job where he had to pre-test the competitions in a programme called Beat the Clock. It was the sort of entertainment programme where members of the audience had to perform certain tasks at high speed within a limited period of time, e.g. catch as many tennis-balls as possible with a stove-pipe. The trial runs before the live programmes were always done by young actors.

Ever since he used to drive his uncle's tractor at Fairmount, James Dean had a passion for fast cars.

They were paid $ 5 per hour. This may not have been a fortune, but, together with other odd jobs, it was enough for Dean to keep his head above water. Frank Heller, a CBS television producer, remembers that whenever Dean was not acting in a television play, he used to master the most difficult games in Beat the Clock and that he had complete control of his body. The reason was probably that when he was a boy in Fairmount he had learned all kinds of tricks with the tractors and also how to do exercises on a trapeze which his uncle had built. After losing two front teeth and having to wear a brace, he must have been a little bit more careful to avoid such casualties in the future.

Dean had been recommended to Heller by the agent Elinor Kilgallen, a sister of the columnist Dorothy Kilgallen, whose early death has aroused much speculation: there was a theory that it might have had something to do with the assassination of John F. Kennedy, that it was all part of a larger conspiracy in which Lee Oswald was by no means the only culprit. Elinor Kilgallen had insisted that unless he took him on, she would refuse to supply a single good actor again, pointing out that Dean would be "a great star" one day. So his road to success had been paved to a large extent by television. However, James Dean was not the only star who rose from the position of odd job man with the

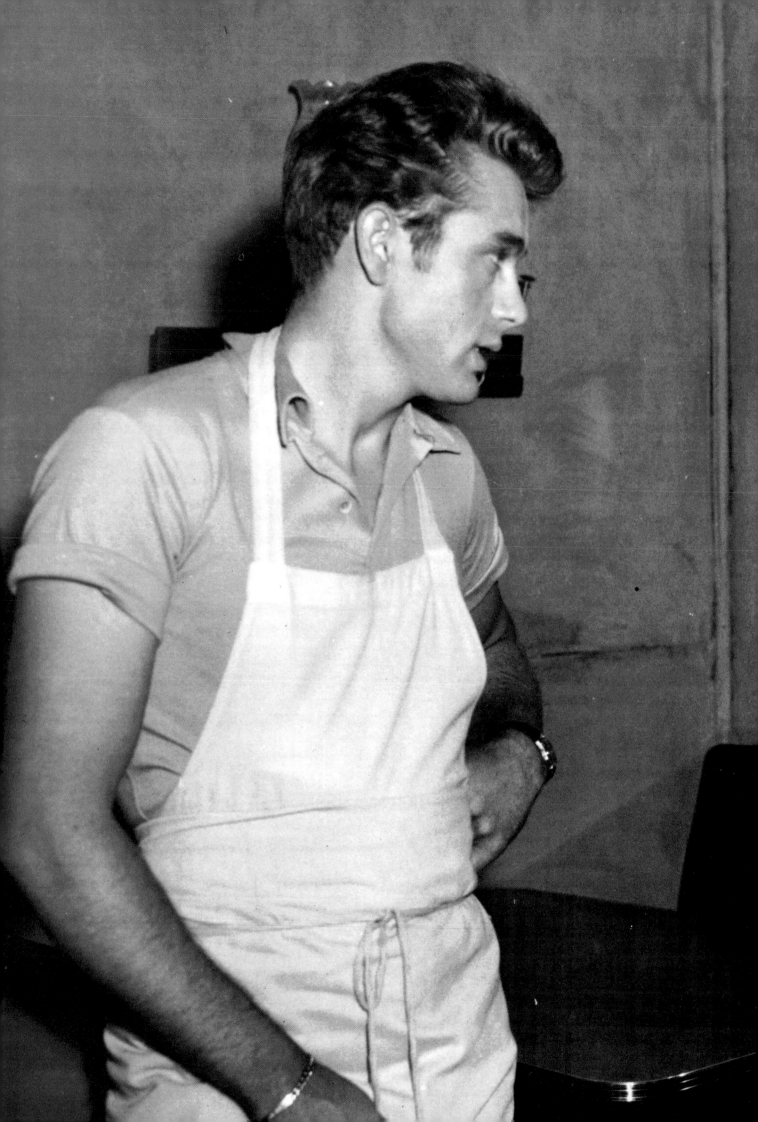

television to the dizzy heights of stardom. There were plenty of others, such as Jack Lemmon, Grace Kelly, Paul Newman, Charlton Heston and Lee Marvin, who were being discovered at the same time and who owed their success mainly to the opportunities given to them by television. And they all eventually outgrew the limited dimensions of the television screen.

Dean did not, of course, continue to do odd jobs for long. At that time, at the beginning of the fifties, live television and radio plays were extremely popular, and Dean was given roles more and more often. This was also the time when he met Bill Bast again and shared with him the philosophy he had learned from Antoine de Saint-Exupéry: "The essence is invisible to the eye."

Until now he had been too much concerned with the sheer struggle for survival and there had been very little time for learning and studying. He had been gaining a lot of experience, but only in a rather haphazard, unsystematic way. Although he had been devouring enormous quantities of books, he was probably rather worried when he presented himself for the entrance exam at the Actors' Studio as one among 150 candidates. But when he had to audition under Lee and Molly Strasberg's critical eyes, he passed with flying colours. However, James Dean did not go to

lessons very regularly. One reason was that he had to work to earn some money, but he also felt that he already knew their methods from his days with the theatre group in Hollywood and that he was talented enough to put into practice what he had learned without practising too much.

After a series of jobs outside the world of the stage, he was finally given a role in a theatre play called See the Jaguar. After a few trial runs in Connecticut it was eventually performed in New York in December 1952, but was torn to pieces by the critics. After only six performances it was decided that it should be discontinued. But there was some comfort for Dean: his acting of young Wally Wilkins was described as being extraordinarily good.

James Dean acquired an image of an angry young man, although this did not always make him very popular with his colleagues. Here in "Rebel Without a Cause".

Pages 20/21: James Dean with Pat Hardy while rehearsing for the SCHLITZ PLAYHOUSE OF STARS: "The Unlighted Road", a play which is said to be one of his most popular television programmes. After his death it was repeated by NBC five times within a relatively short time.

As a result he was offered more and more television roles, with an increasing number of television films. But some of his live plays were also recorded. This was not usually done at the time because magnetic recording had not been invented and so it was a rather complicated and difficult process to preserve live programmes for posterity. Nevertheless, a few ingenious people had the clever idea to make so-called cinescopes of the programmes, i.e. to record them straight from a monitoring screen while they were on the air. Although the quality was obviously rather mediocre, it was decided at this early stage of television that cinescopes were acceptable enough to help bridge the time gap between the East and the West coast of the States. A programme could be recorded live in New York and a few days later shown again at an equally respectable time in the evening on the West coast. This was done with television and radio plays in the States and it explains why quite a number of Dean's television performances can still be watched today. As soon as he had become famous, in fact, a number of his television plays were repeated regularly, including among others his enactment of John the Evangelist.

James Dean with an air of melancholy in his eyes. A very moving portrait.

By now his television plays were beginning to attract whole baskets full of mail from female admirers, and even Hollywood began to take an interest in this angry young man who had been modelling his art on actors like Marlon Brando and Montgomery Clift. He would even use mannerisms of the two famous actors. It is a well-known fact that he found out Clift's ex-directory telephone number and used to give him a ring every now and then just to hear his voice and then use it in his own acting. And he did the same with Marlon Brando. It is even said that he signed some of his letters as "James (Brando-Clift) Dean". Dean's fame finally reached Hollywood and he was given a number of auditions for several films. But before Hollywood could embrace this non-conformist, up-and-coming young star, he was given a chance to say good-bye to New York by taking a role in André Gide's play The Immoralist, a Broadway version of his early autobiographical novel about homosexuality. The rehearsals presented something of a problem because of his changing moods which often created a bad atmosphere. In the end, however, the test performance in Philadelphia went very smoothly, and the première was praised sky-high by the critics. When it came to New York, one of the dress rehearsals was seen by the playwright Paul Osborn who was writing the script for the film version of East of Eden. He immediately suggested to

James Dean during a phone-call at one of the Warner Bros. offices. Later this photo served as a subject for a poster advertising the less successful musical "Dean".

Elia Kazan that he should have a look at this young chap. Kazan did and felt that Dean was in fact the ideal actor to play Cal Trask.

This was the beginning of Dean's Hollywood career. A number of difficulties still had to be overcome, because it was felt that Dean was a bit of an unknown quantity for such a massive undertaking. However, all doubts were dispersed as soon as the studio bosses had seen some trial shots of several scenes, and everybody was convinced that Kazan would definitely produce another hit. One of the trial shots, in which James Dean played together with Richard Davalos, had to be deleted from the final version because it was felt that the scene between the twin brothers could be understood homosexually. Such scenes, including his role as a gay Arabic servant in The Immoralist, as well as his interest in Marlon Brando and Montgomery Clift, may have been the reason why people often thought that he was homosexual or at least bisexual. However, the only relationships of his which are documented in any way are the ones with girl-friends and his unhappy love affair with the Italian actress Pier Angeli, in whom he began to take an interest in Hollywood.

Dean had got to know Pier Angeli while he was right in the thick of working on East of Eden. As before, he had bought

27

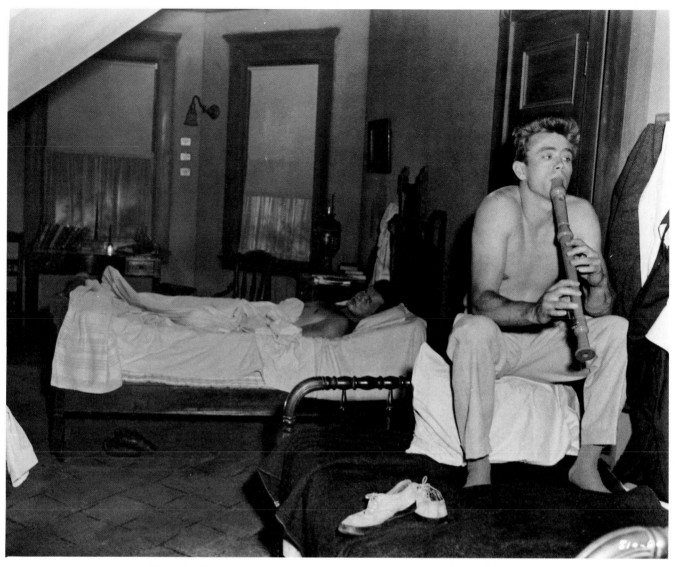

"East of Eden", with Richard Davalos. This scene was not used in the film.

himself a heavy motorbike, but Elia Kazan had succeeded in dissuading him from riding to outside shots on it. He rather liked the idea that Dean should take quarters in the changing room so that he could keep him under control. During a break he went next door, where the film The Silver Chalice was being shot, to say hello to Paul Newman and Joseph Wiseman whom he knew from his television days in New York. This was when he met Pier Angeli, then 21 years old, who was also acting in the film. The two fell in love with one another, much to the displeasure of Pier Angeli's mother.

Fiction vs reality: a studio portrait of James Dean as a film star and in private. His face, in the shadow of a flashlight, has been retouched considerably, but it is not a very favourable picture of him.

When East of Eden was finished in 1954, James Dean was contemplating marriage. He went to New York for two weeks, to take part in a television programme, but when he came back to Hollywood, he discovered that their relationship had gone stale. A few months later, in October, Pier Angeli announced her engagement to the singer Vic Damone. Dean was thunderstruck. He immediately tried to distract himself with the pleasures of life and had one

28

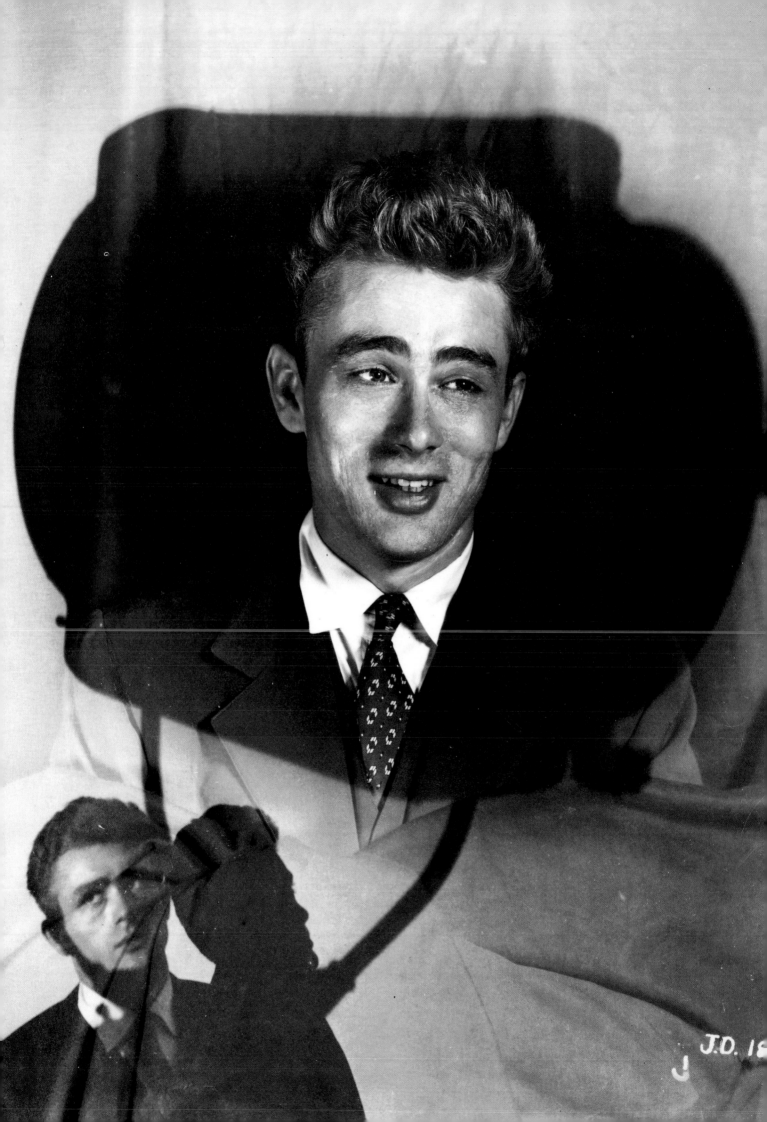

girl-friend after another, changing them at least as frequently as he had in New York. The studio management felt that what was going on in his living quarters was a bit on the dubious side, and so he was asked to vacate the premises and find a home elsewhere.

When East of Eden made its way into the cinemas, the critics went mad with enthusiasm. Dean had really become a star now. However, he had absolutely no intention of joining in the press campaign to market his film, and so he made it known that he was not only an actor, but also good at car racing. Warner Brothers gave Dean a long-term contract which included 9 films within 6 years and a guaranteed income of $ 15 000 per film. Should the opportunity arise, he was to be given the chance to perform at the Broadway. So far as television programmes were concerned, he was allowed to plan them in, provided they did not clash with the film production timetable.

It soon became obvious that his next job should be the main role in the film Rebel Without a Cause. Film producer Nicholas Ray did not want any other actor for this role, and went out of his way to create an atmosphere of trust in which James Dean, who was rather a shy person in private, felt that he would be able to give of his best. Shortly before beginning his work on the film and against the will of

the studio mangement, Dean took part in two car races at Palm Springs with his Porsche. In the first race he came first, and in the second one – which consisted not only of amateurs but also professionals – he came third.

Nicholas Ray even had a knack of coping with Dean's mood .These moods used to make the actor unpopular with most people around him, expecially the technical staff. But Ray knew how to inspire Dean to live the scenes as if they were real. It was Dean himself who actually suggested that a knife scene should be filmed without the use of stuntmen and with real flick knives. The outcome was a film which indoubtedly tells us more about Dean as a person than any other film and which gives us a key to his character.

In his private life Dean did his best to be difficult. He completely ignored the jet set, and he was not prepared to waste his time fooling around with press conferences. Warner Brothers, however, did not want to share this new star in their sky with any of the other film companies, and so the next film was planned as quickly as possible: Giant.

It was estimated that the film would cost approximately $ 5 million, so it hardly comes as a surprise when we learn that George Stevens, the film director and co-producer, advised Dean not to

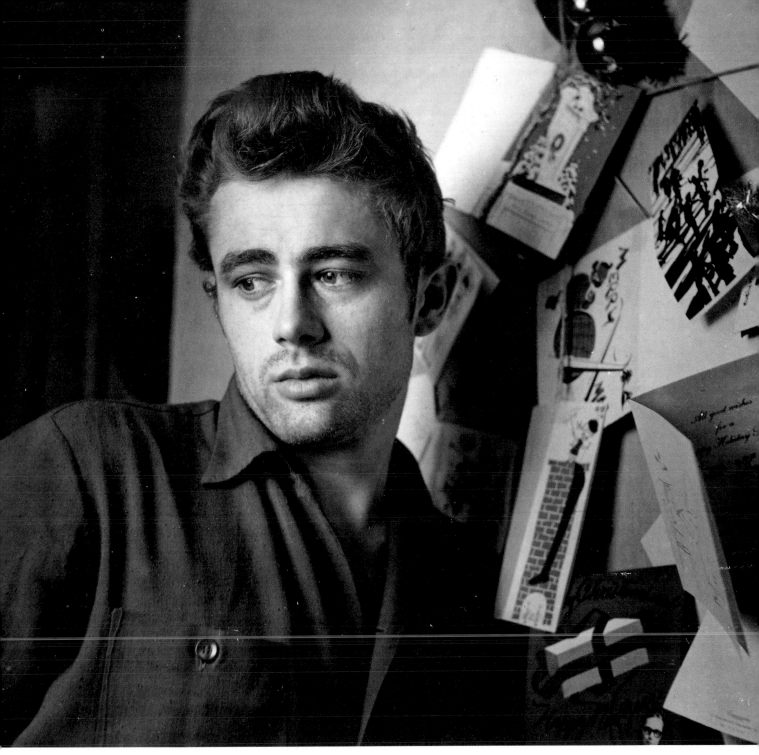

James Dean with Christmas cards.

participate in any car races while the film was being made. Dean agreed, but could not resist the temptation to take part in a car race in Santa Barbara, after the filming had already started. His own first scene, though, was not scheduled until several weeks after the beginning of the work. The filming was not quite as relaxed this time as it had been with Elia Kazan and Nicholas Ray. Stevens did not think much of long discussion with the actors or even improvising, and this made the atmosphere rather tense. Dean not only quarrelled with the director, but also refused to avoid arguments with his colleagues. Dennis Hopper and Eliza-

beth Taylor were the only actors who were on good terms with him, mainly because they did not always agree with Steven's demands either.

After the filming of the outside scenes the rest of the film was shot in the Hollywood studios. It was during this time that the relationship between Dean and Stevens deteriorated even further and Liz Taylor had to go into hospital twice. Perhaps Stevens was too much of a father figure for Dean so that he felt rebellious against the older man. A few years later Liz Taylor used to say that Stevens had in fact appreciated and respected Dean's acting and that he just had not been able to communicate his appreciation. It seems that the whole situation was a version of Trask's family drama in <u>East of Eden</u>.

James Dean with his first Porsche.

James Dean could spend hours playing his Bongo drum and forgetting the world around him.

Dean's favourite image of himself: always ready for a race.

Shortly before the end of the filming of <u>Giant</u> James Dean bought a Porsche 550 Spyder to take part in a race in Salinas. As soon as the work was finished, Dean decided to drive the car to the racing-track himself, rather than having it delivered by a lorry. This was on 30 September 1955. His number, 130, had been painted on the car in big letters, and he was accompanied by his car mechanic Rolf Wütherich. Their trip came to a sudden end when, at 5.45 that afternoon, Dean's car ran into another car at a junction. The other driver, Donald Turnupseed, was a student. James Dean died immediately, whereas his mechanic got jerked out of the car and had to be nursed in hospital for several months, and the student got off with no more than bad shock. What exactly led to this accident at the junction of roads 466 and 41 is impossible to say. Quite probably, he simply did not see the other vehicle because the sun was shining into his eyes.

James Dean and Juliet Harris at a rehearsal for "East of Eden". Dean seems to be doing his duty rather absent-mindedly.

34

JAMES DEAN

JENSEITS VON EDEN

Ein Farbfilm der Warner Bros.
A Warner Communications Company
im Verleih der Warner-Columbia

Fernsehprogramm vom 28. August mit 3. September · 35. Woche 1965 · Nummer 35 80 Pfennig · öS. 5,— · sfr. —,90 · Lire 150,— A 1917

BRAVO

mit
Rundfunk-Programm
von Radio Luxemburg

Die bittere
Wahrheit

Der Tag
an dem
James Dean
starb

James Dean

Pages 36/37: James Dean as Cal Trask searching fo his roots in "East of Eden". Bette Treadville, who plays the barmaid, is showing him where he will find the ansers to his question about the past.

After his death James Dean remained a favourite topic in teenage magazines all over the world. This is the title page of a West German magazine called Bravo, announcing "The bitter truth: the day James Dean died."

Although Dean was already dead, the ambulance men tried to revive him by means of an oxygen mask. This may be the reason why there were so many rumours in subsequent years that he had not died at all but seized the opportunity to get away from Hollywood and the inland revenue.

But James Dean's death was only the beginning of his career as a cultic idol. His funeral at Fairmount Cemetry at 2 p.m. on 8 October 1955 marked the beginning of a cult which, until then, had only been accorded to Rudolph Valentino and was repeated again later with Elvis Presley. Again and again pieces of masonry were broken off his gravestone, and a bronze bust of James Dean, which had been put at the entrance of the cemetery, was stolen several months later. And it still happens that flowers and wreaths are laid at his grave.

James Dean is said to have made the following statement: "I believe there is only one real form of greatness for a person, and that is bridging the gap between life and death. If someone manages to live on after death, then he may have been a great man. For me the only kind of success or greatness ... is immortality."

He had certainly achieved his ambition even before his sudden death.

James Dean's Career

James Dean's public life started with school performances when he was still a boy. However, this list only includes his professional apperances on T.V. and radio as well as in films and on the stage. It all began with an advertising spot for Pepsi Cola. The dates of television programmes are the dates when they were first broadcast.

February 1950

T.V. advertising spot for Pepsi Cola.

March 1950

Hill Number One
This is a special television broadcast for Easter, in which James Dean plays a minor role, that of John the Evangelist.

1951

Beat the Clock
James Dean himself does not actually appear in this New York entertainment programme, but he is one of the actors who, before the live broadcast, took part in trial runs for the various competitions between members of the audience.

James Dean's image demanded that he should look pensive. But there were times when he had quite a michievous twinkle in his eyes.

Sailor, Beware!
A Paramount comedy.
Directed by Hal Walker.
Cast includes: Dean Martin, Jerry Lewis, Corinne Calvert, Marion Marshall.
James Dean's part only consists of three lines, but his scenes are cut out again.

Fixed Bayonets
A 20th Century Fox war film.
Directed by Samuel Fuller.
Cast includes: Richard Basehart, Gene Evans, Michael O'Shea, Richard Hylton.
James plays a minor role in which he has to report in only one line that the scout party has arrived back.

1952

Has Anybody Seen My Gal?
Universal film.
Directed by Douglas Sirk.

Cast includes Charles Coburn, Rock Hudson, Piper Laurie, Lynn Bari, William Reynolds.

As before, James Dean's role is very short. All he has to do is say to Charles Coburn: "Hey, Gramps, I'll have a choc malt, heavy on the choc, plenty of milk, four spoons of malt, two scoops of vanilla ice cream, one mixed with the rest and one floating."

CBS Radio Workshop (CBS)
Alias Jane Doe (CBS)
Stars over Hollywood (CBS)
The Adventures of Sam Spade (CBS)
These are four series of radio plays in which James Dean takes several minor roles.

United States Steel Hours
"Prologue to Glory" – 11 May 1952, ABC

Women of Trachis
This is a new translation by Ezra Pound of a play by Sophocles. James Dean takes a role in the theatre play at the New School for Social Research.

To get roles as an actor, James Dean needed among other things some expressive portrait photographs of himself.

Tales of Tomorrow (ABC)
Treasury Men in Action (NBC)
Martin Kane, Private Eye (NBC)
Campbell Sound Stage (NBC)
Danger (CBS)
Kraft Television Theater (NBC)
In each of these television series James Dean plays minor parts in some programmes.

The Metamorphosis
In August 1952 Dean reads a dramatized version of Kafka's short story at the Village Theater.

See the Jaguar
A three-act play by Richard Nash.
Directed by Michael Gordon.
Cast includes: Phillip Pine, David Clarke, Constance Ford, Roy Fant, Margaret Barker, Arthur Kennedy, James Dean (playing the mute Wally Wilkins).
After a trial première in Philadelphia on 3 December 1952, the play is shown at the Open Court Broadway Theater but is taken off after only six performances.

1953

The Kate Smith Hour
"Hound of Heaven" – 15 January 1953 (NBC)

Treasury Men in Action
"The Case of the Watchful Dog" – 29 January 1953 (NBC)

Many of the television plays in which Dean acted were about life and death. This is a scene from "Death is My Neighbor", a programme in the CBS series Danger, with Walter Hampden and Betsy Palmer.

Danger

"No Room" – 14 April 1953 (NBC)
James Dean plays with Martin Kingsley and Irene Vernon.

Treasury Men in Action

"The Case of the Sawed-Off Shotgun" 16 April 1953 (NBC)

The Campbell Television Soundstage

"Something for an Empty Briefcase" – 18 July 1953 (NBC)

Studio One Summer Theater

"Sentence of Death" – 17 August 1953 (CBS)
Dean plays with Thomas Walsh and Adrienne Spies.

Danger

"Death is My Neighbor" – 25 August 1953 (CBS)
James Dean plays with Betsy Palmer and Walter Hampden.

Danger

"The Little Woman" – August 1953 (CBS)

The Big Story

11 September 1953 (NBC)
Like all the other programmes in this television series, it is the story around one of the newspaper headlines of the day.

Omnibus
4 October 1953 (CBS)
This experimental television series consists of plays followed by discussions on topical subjects. Alistair Cooke acts as compère, and in this programme Dean plays with Hume Cronyn, Jessica Tandy, Carol Channing and Elliot Reed.

Kraft Television Theater
"Keep Our Honor Bright" – 14 October 1953 (NBC)

Campbell Television Soundstage
"Life Sentence" – 16 October 1953 (NBC)

Kraft Television Theater
"A Long Time Till Dawn" – 11 November 1953 (NBC)

The Armstrong Circle Theater
"The Bells of Cockaigne" – 17 November 1953 (NBC)

Robert Montgomery Presents
"Harvest" – 23 November 1953 (NBC)
In this special programme for Thanksgiving James Dean plays with Dorothy Gish and Vaughan Taylor.

1954

The Immoralist
A three-act play by Ruth and Augustus Goetz.
After a novel by André Gide.

Directed by Daniel Mann.
Cast includes: Geraldine Page (Marcelline), John Heldabrand (Dr. Robert), Charles Dingle (Bocage), Louis Jourdan (Michel), James Dean (Bachir), Paul Huber (Dr. Garrin), Adelaide Klein (Sidma), David J. Stewart (Moktir), Billy Gunn (Dolit).
Première at the Royal Theater, Broadway, on 1 February 1954. James Dean has been quarrelling with the producer, Billy Rose, ever since the provincial trial performances because he feels that he is being criticized too much. So after only two weeks he gets his revenge by withdrawing from the play.

East of Eden
Filming starts in Hollywood in May 1954 and finishes on 5 August of the same year. Further details in the chapter His Films.

The Philco Television Playhouse
"Run Like a Thief" – 5 September 1954 (NBC)

Pages 46/47: Aron (Richard Davalos) in "East of Eden" does not know yet that his twin brother Cal (Dean) has better chances with his girl-friend Abra (Julie Harris) than anyone would expect. This scene gives a good impression of the conflict between family ties and adolescent love.

Danger
"Padlocks" – 9 November 1954 (NBC)

Dean's partner in this programme of the series is Mildred Dunnock.

The General Electric Theater
"The Dark, Dark Hour" – December 1954 (CBS)

The compère in this television series is Ronald Reagan. Like Alfred Hitchcock in his series, he says a few words at the beginning and end of each programme. In this particular programme, however, Reagan is also one of the actors, together with James Dean.

The General Electric Theater
"I Am a Fool" – December 1954 (CBS)
Dean's partners are Natalie Wood and Eddie Albert.

1955

United States Steel Hour
"The Thief" – 4 January 1955 (ABC)
Dean plays with Paul Lukas, Diana Lynn, Mary Astor and Patrick Knowles. While the studio technicians have no problems in following the dialogues through the studio microphones, Mary Astor and Paul Lukas have great difficulties because even when he is some distance away, James Dean speaks so softly that they can hardly hear him. The older stars are quite amazed when, after the broadcast, Dean's acting is mentioned particularly favourably by the critics.

The Lux Video Theater
"The Life of Emile Zola" – 14 March 1955 (NBC)
The programme is followed by a live interview with James Dean.

Rebel Without a Cause
Filming starts in Hollywood in March 1955 and finishes on 3 May 1955. Further details in the chapter His Films.

East of Eden
Cinema première on 9 April 1955.

Schlitz Playhouse of Stars
"The Unlighted Road" – 6 May 1955 (CBS)
Dean plays with Pat Hardy, Murvyn Vye, Robert Williams and Charles Wagenheim.

Giant
Filming starts in May 1955, but James Dean's work does not start until 3 June. The filming finishes on 5 September 1955, a few weeks before Dean's fatal car accident. Further details about the film in the chapter His Films.

TV spot on road safety
While he is still working on Giant, James Dean takes part in an advertising

This is James Dean's "Giant" outfit (here with Elizabeth Taylor), in which he also appeared in T.V. spots on road safety.

spot on road safety. Dressed in his <u>Giant</u> cowboy outfit, he says to Gig Young, "I take my chances on a racing track any day, rather than on a highway". And when Dean gets up and turns towards the door, Gig Young asks him if there is any advice he might want to give him. "Take it easy, driving, you know," says Dean, "the life you might save might be mine." What happened a few weeks later makes you wonder if he and the other young driver had really listened to these words.

Rebel Without a Cause
Cinema première on 29 October 1955.

Giant
Cinema première on 10 October 1956.

Pages 50/51: James Dean as an exponent of the generation gap, quarrelling with Raymond Massey as his father in "East of Eden".

Illustrierte
film-Bühne
Nr. 2828

(EAST OF EDEN)

Jenseits von Eden

EIN CinemaScopE -FILM IN WARNERCOLOR

His Films

Today's James Dean cult is limited to the three main films in which he played the main roles. Due to his untimely death, his actual career only lasted for a very short time, and only very few of his television plays have been recorded. The ones that do still exist show James Dean in relatively minor roles, so to gain an impression of his acting one would have to look at a large number of very short scenes. In this chapter we shall therefore concentrate exclusively on his three well-known films. It is hoped that the reader will feel inspired to find out more about James Dean and to take an interest in the publications, pictures and video films that are readily available. For a better understanding of the following data please note that the order of the actors as well as of the backstage staff follows the credits of the German version of each film. In addition, however, we have also listed the names of the characters side by side with those of each actor. There are additional notes and comments which should be self-explanatory.

Poster for "East of Eden".

53

1955
East of Eden

This poster for "East of Eden" shows how much Dean's status as a film star had increased since the première of that film. While he is still only mentioned as the second actor in the credits, he is number one on this poster.

Warner Bros. Pictures
presents
EAST OF EDEN
after a novel by John Steinbeck.
An Elia Kazan Production.

Julie Harris	Abra
James Dean	Cal Trask
Raymond Massey	Adam Trask
Burl Ives	Sheriff Sam
Richard Davalos	Aron Trask
Jo Van Fleet	Kate
Albert Dekker	Will Hamilton
Lois Smith	Anne
Harold Gordon	Mr Albrecht
Nick Dennis	Rantani

A CinemaScope Film

Film Editor	Owen Marks, A.C.E.
Sound Editor	Stanley Jones
Stage Manager	George James Hopkins
German Version	Deutsche Mondial Film GmbH
Musical Director	Leonard Rosenman
Screenplay by	Paul Osborn
Directed by	Elia Kazan

The credits are followed by a text on the screen expressing the idea of a dark and somber wall formed by the Santa Lucia Mountains (Northern California) which separate the peaceful little town of Salinas from the lively fishing port of Monterey, 20 miles away.

Further actors who are not mentioned in the credits: Richard Garrick (Dr. Edwards), Timothy Carey (Joe), Lonny Chapman (Roy), Barbara Baxley (nurse), Bette Treadville (barmaid), Tex Mooney (barman), Harry Cording (chucker-out), Loretta Rush (ticket seller), Bill Phillips (coalman), Mario Siletti (Piscora), Jonathan Haze (Piscora's son), Jack Carr, Roger Creed, Effie Laird, Wheaton Chambers, Ed Clark, Al Ferguson, Franklyn Farnum, Rose Plummer (fair ground staff), John George (photographer), C. Ramsey Hill (British officer), Edward McNally (soldier), Earle Hodgins (owner of a shooting-gallery).

The film is of John Steinbeck's novel with the same name, published by Viking Press, New York, 1952 (602 pages).

JAMES DEAN

IN SEINEM UNVERGESSLICHEN WELTERFOLG

JENSEITS VON EDEN

(EAST OF EDEN)

JULIE HARRIS · RAYMOND MASSEY

NACH DEM GLEICHNAMIGEN ROMAN VON JOHN STEINBECK

REGIE: ELIA KAZAN

EIN FILM DER WARNER BROS. IN WarnerColor UND CinemaScope

Running times: 115 minutes. Colour: Warner-Color. Format: CinemaScope. Filmed from May to August 1954.
Première: 9 April 1955
In the German version of the credits director of photography Ted McCord was left out by mistake. Actor Harold Gordon was listed as Harold Cordon, and the first name of the stage manager George was misspelt Georges, i.e. like the French name.

Summary:

"East of Eden is an American saga: a historical documentary spanning the time from the American Civil War until World War I. The author tells the story of the Trask familiy – Adam, the father, the twin brothers Cal and Aron, and their unfaithful mother Kate." This is how the German paperback edition summarizes John Steinbeck's novel.

The words "Monterey 1917", which appear on the screen at the end of the credits, tell the audience immediately that the novel has been cut down to the proportions of a single period in history. This period, however, follows the original novel fairly accurately. The introductory text corresponds to a longer passage in the novel which begins with the words. "The Salinas Valley is in Northern California. It is a long narrow swale between two ranges of mountains, and the Salinas River winds and twists up the center until it falls at last into Monterey Bay." There is no reference to the Santa Lucia Mountains until the paragraph after the next, which is quite a long one: "They were dark and brooding – unfriendly and dangerous."

An important aspect of Steinbeck's novel is the setting and its effect on the lives and moods of the characters. In the film this particular theme is not exploited and does not go any further than the short screen text at the beginning, even though the scenery is of course always present. The problems that occur are more a result of the relationships between the characters and not so much of their environment.

Above: Dean's role as Cal Trask turned him into a film star overnight.

Below: Cal Trask has a bad surprise for his twin brother Aron: Kate, their mother, is still alive!

Cal (Dean) and Abra (Julie Harris) at the fairground. They are getting more and more fond of each other.

Pages 60/61: Harry Cording, the chucker-out at Kate's bar, prevents Cal's first meeting with his mother.

Cal Trask (Dean) in search of his lost mother in Monterey.

The title of the film is shown against the background of the mountains which are mentioned in the text. Then the camera pans towards the sea and, with a sudden change of scenery, Monterey comes into view, showing a woman veiled in black walking along. The camera follows her and then focuses on James Dean who,

filling the whole screen, is seen sitting beside the road and following the woman with his eyes. James Dean, in his role as Cal Trask, has a problem: his father, Adam Trask, seems to prefer Cal's twin brother Aron. Aron is a very obedient son and always complies with his father's wishes. He willingly helps him with a rescue operation in which blocks of ice are used to transport vegetables in the summer heat. Cal, on

59

Cal's first step into a new world: Kate's brothel.

the other hand, appears to be somewhat unreliable at times and is often pushed aside.

Adam Trask is blindly infatuated with his altruistic son Aron, because he feels that his paternal love is reciprocated by him. On the other hand, he regards Cal as a dead loss, not realizing that this other son of his has far more of a yearning to be loved by his dad than Aron. Cal feels like an outcast and does everything in his power to win his father's love or at least his respect, but never quite manages to live up to his expectations and is therefore regarded as a rebel, the black sheep in the family.

It is obviously because of his father's favouritism and preference of Aron that Cal feels resentful. But why did Adam Trask bring up his sons on his own? He himself says that their mother died shortly after the twins were born, but Cal has found out that she is in fact

Cal's fight with Mr. Hamilton (Albert Dekker) marks the beginning of his large-scale speculation in beans.

alive. What is more, he is convinced that she is living in the neighbouring village and that she is the rich proprietress of a certain house which is never talked about in public but which is said to be open to all men. Cal now believes that he has found the reason for his "bad" character: Aron takes after his father, whereas he himself is more akin to his brothel-owning mother.

However, Cal would not be the son of his rather strict father, if he now gave up all hope of ever gaining his father's recognition. Cal sees an opportunity when Adam Trask loses his fortune. In spite of plenty of ice, a whole railway waggon load of lettuce is spoilt; the ice has melted in the scorching heat, thus creating hot-house temperatures in the waggon and effectively destroying the entire crop. It is 1917, and the States are about to enter into the world war which is raging at the moment. Cal thinks that the impending war can be turned into

Under the eyes of the sheriff (Burl Ives) Aron (Richard Davalos) begins to discover his true feelings for Abra (Julie Harris).

JAMES DEAN
in seinem unvergeßlichen Welterfolg
JENSEITS VON EDEN
(EAST OF EDEN)
JULIE HARRIS   RAYMOND MASSEY
REGIE: ELIA KAZAN

profit by speculating in beans and that the ensuing success could make up for his father's losses. In this way he is hoping to gain his father's love. To put his plan into practice, Cal needs an enormous amount of money, which he borrows from his mother. She gives to him willingly because she sees a certain affinity between herself and her son.

Abra, a girl who is in love with Aron, shows a lot of sympathy for Cal. She somehow realizes that Cal is undervalued and misunderstood by his family. She can see how much he is longing to be loved by his father, and she is convinced that Cal's plans to restore his father's wealth will be successful. So she helps him in the preparations for his father's birthday party. Cal's speculative business has been successful, and this is the occasion when he wants to hand over the money, hoping that such a birthday present will enable him to gain final recognition from his father.

But Cal and Abra's plan goes completely wrong. Aron's birthday surprise consists of announcing his engagement with Abra. Adam Trask at first stubbornly refuses to open Cal's birthday present, and when he sees all the money he reacts with suspicion. Unable to see the intention behind it, he asks where his badly brought-up son got it from, and when he is told, he calls his son a war-profiteer and demands that he should pay the money back to all those who have been tricked.

The beautiful house of cards which Cal built has collapsed with a crash. Extremely hurt and disappointed, he rushes out of the house. Abra follows him, and so does his "dear" brother Aron, on whom Cal turns and vents the painful frustration which has been building up inside him over the many years of a hapless and loveless existence. He does so by telling him plainly and bluntly the truth about their mother. But whereas Cal was able to cope with this information and even to use it creatively and in a positive way, Aron just cracks up. Until now, problems have always been kept away from him, and the news about his mother is so overwhelming that he immediately decides to get completely drunk and then to enlist in the army where he is accepted at once.

When Adam Trask finds out, he suffers a severe stroke. But the only people who are around to look after him are Cal and Abra, while his favourite son Aron is far away. What is more, Abra has now discovered that she loves Cal and that she would like to belong to him. There is a forceful scene at father's sickbed, in which the paralyzed old man weakly clasps his son's hand, thus letting him know at long last that he values and loves him and that he is happy to be looked after by him from now on. In spite of the turbulence, inner strife and lovelessness in Cal's life, it is he who turns out to be the more stable and dependable one of the two twins.

The final glimpse of the Trasks is that of Cal sitting beside his father's bed, in a dark room.

James Dean's role as Cal Trask is rightly regarded as one of the most impressive dramatic achievements of the fifties. At one fell swoop it turned him into the most prominent spokesman of the rebellious youth of the time. Although Dean probably managed to play his role more convincing than any of the other actors, his colleagues also acted extremely well so that the film is of a high standard throughout. The critics of the time rather felt that Dean's acting was too much like that of Marlon Brando, but they recognized that it was mainly due to Dean that "all in all it left a moving and memorable impression." If Dean had been a little insecure at the beginning of the filming, he gradually

You can't buy love with money, says Raymond Massey to James Dean, who plays his son in this film.

Pages 68/69: Despite their problems with the older generation, everything ends happily for Julie Harris and James Dean.

JAMES DEAN
in seinem unvergeßlichen Welterfolg

JENSEITS VON EDEN

(EAST OF EDEN)

JULIE HARRIS   RAYMOND MASSEY

REGIE: ELIA KAZAN

became more and more self-confident as the work progressed, thanks to Kazan's encouraging help as a director. By the end of the film he had definitely become a star. It is also worth noting that Dean was expressing part of himself in this role, and part of his difficult relationship with his own father.

Nevertheless, it is not only James Dean's dramatic achievement, or even that of his colleagues, which makes for the dramatic impact of the film. To a very large exent, the intense atmosphere is due to the masterful expertise of the director, Elia Kazan and also the resourceful inventiveness of the camera crew. The full force and significance of the dialogues between father and son are emphasized by the way in which the camera focuses on the two people from an angle behind them.

In addition to these highly dramatic scenes of internal and external conflict, there are also some very tender love scenes, showing James Dean and Julie Harris in a meadow of yellow flowers. These are some of the lasting impressions of the film.

Thanks to video cassettes "East of Eden" is now available at any time. The scenes of Julie Harris and James Dean in a flowery meadow provide good advertising material.

A poster for Dean's second great film, "Rebel Without a Cause".

Illustrierte Film-Bühne

Nr. 3211

JAMES DEAN
IN

...denn sie wissen nicht, was sie tun

(REBEL WITHOUT A CAUSE)

EIN CINemaScopE-FILM IN WARNERCOLOR

1955
Rebel Without a Cause

Warner Bros. Pictures Presents
James Dean in
Rebel Without a Cause.

Cast includes

Natalie Wood	Judy
Sal Mineo	Plato
Jim Backus	Jim's father
and	
Ann Doran	Jim's mother
Corey Allen	Buzz
William Hopper	Judy's father
Rochelle Hudson	Judy's mother
Dennis Hopper	Goon
Edward Platt	Probation Officer
Steffi Sidney	Mil
Marietta Canty	Plato's maid
Virginia Brissac	Jim's grandmother
Beverly Long	Helen
Ian Wolfe	Teacher
Frank Mazzola	Crunch
Robert Foulk	Gene
Jack Simmons	Cookie
Tom Bernard	Harry
Nick Adams	Moose
Jack Grinnage	Chick
Clifford Morris	Cliff

A film by
Warner Bros. First National
in CinemaScope and Warner Color

Screenplay by	Steward Stern
After the novel by	Nicholas Ray
Director of photography	Ernest Haller, A.S.C.
Artistic director	Malcolm Brett
Film editor	William Ziegler
Sound editor	Stanley Jones
Stage manager	William Wallace
Wardrobe	Moss Mabry
Make-up	Gordon Bau, S.M.A.
Assistant directors	Don Page
	Robert Farfan
German version	Deutsche Mondial Film GmbH
Musical director	Leonard Rosen-man
Produced by	David Weisbart
Directed by	Nicholas Ray

A poster for "Rebel Without a Cause".

72

JAMES DEAN · NATALIE WOOD

...denn sie wissen nicht, was sie tun

Rebell Without A Cause

Regie: NICHOLAS RAY · Ein Farbfilm der WARNER BROS. in WARNERCOLOR und CinemaScope

Other actors who are not mentioned in the credits: Jimmy Baird (Bean), Dick Wessel (Führer), Nelson Leigh (Sergeant), Dorothy Abbot (nurse), Louise Lane (policewoman), House Peters (policeman), Gus Schilling (supervisor), Bruce Noonan (monitor), Almira Sessions (elderly teacher), Peter Miller (gangster), Paul Bryar (sergeant on duty), Robert Williams (Moose's father), David McMahon (Crunch's father).

Running time: 111 minutes. Colour: Warner Color. Format: CinemaScope. Filming from March to May 1955. Pemière: 29 October 1955.

In the German version of the credits, Nicholas Ray was listed as the author of the novel. Actually he designed the basic structure of the plot, which was then developed further by Irving Shulman and turned into a script by Stewart Stern. According to Dimmit's <u>Title Guide to the Talkies</u>, the film was made after the novel <u>Children of the Dark</u> by Irving Shulman, published by Doubleday, Garden City, N.Y., in 1956. The date of publication suggests that Shulman's script pre-dates his novel.

Nicholas Ray, the director, giving James Dean instruction in front of the Griffith Observatory.

Summary:

The film starts with a close-up of a little clockwork monkey jumping about on the floor. Then Jim (played by James Dean) throws himself on the floor so that his face, also focused on in a close-up, becomes visible behind the little monkey. He appears to be slightly tipsy, and as soon as the clockword has run down, he covers the monkey with a piece of cloth. This scene forms the background to the credits. The main action of the film starts with Jim being taken to a police station. His clothes indicate that he comes from a wealthy family, and he is carrying the little monkey in his hand. Then he is put into a cell, to sleep it off.

The following morning Jim's parents come to take him home, and he tells the policeman on duty what made him reach for the bottle: he was worried that he might become as spineless as his henpecked father. This fear has in fact been so obsessive that he has been doing the most extraordinary things. Each time his domineering mother took those escapades as a reason for moving house. She felt that Jim had been unable to make friends in the neighbourhood, and so his mischievous deeds always came as a welcome excuse to persuade her husband to move to a different town.

Pages 76/77: Jim Stark (Dean) and his toy monkey at the police station.

75

Jim's parents are now hopeful that everything will turn out for the best, because they have only just moved to a new town. On the first day at his new school Jim meets "old friends" whom he remembers from his night at the police-station: Judy, Plato and Buzz. Buzz is the leader of a school gang, and he immediately wants to defend his patch against the new intruder and incorporate him into the pecking order. Jim does not want to have any part in it, but after school he cannot avoid getting involved in a fight with flick-knives, in which Buzz wants to "test" the new-comer. Plato, a lone wolf, is the only boy who understands that Jim does not want to avoid the fight out of cowardice, and as he does not want to lose his new friend in an accident, he tries – in vain – to prevent the fight. However, Jim manages to hold his own even without anybody's help.

But this is only the beginning of the conflict between Buzz and Jim. Buzz challenges Jim to a test of strength. The opponents are to drive two stolen cars at high speed towards a steep cliff by the sea and then jump out at the last minute. The person who jumps off first will be branded as a coward. The night before, Jim tries to discuss the matter with his father and to get his advice. But dad is not particularly enamoured of the whole idea. Neither does he understand what it is that Jim wants to prove to himself and

Jim and Buzz (Corey Allen) fighting with knives. In a number of countries this scene was censored.

A pensive moment for James Dean and Corey Allen before their test of strength.

others and why he should want to prove anything to anyone. And so he does not succeed in convincing his son that such a show of strength would be wrong.

On the night of the contest the cars of their classmates are lined up respectfully on either side, their headlights casting an uncanny glare on the whole scene. Buzz

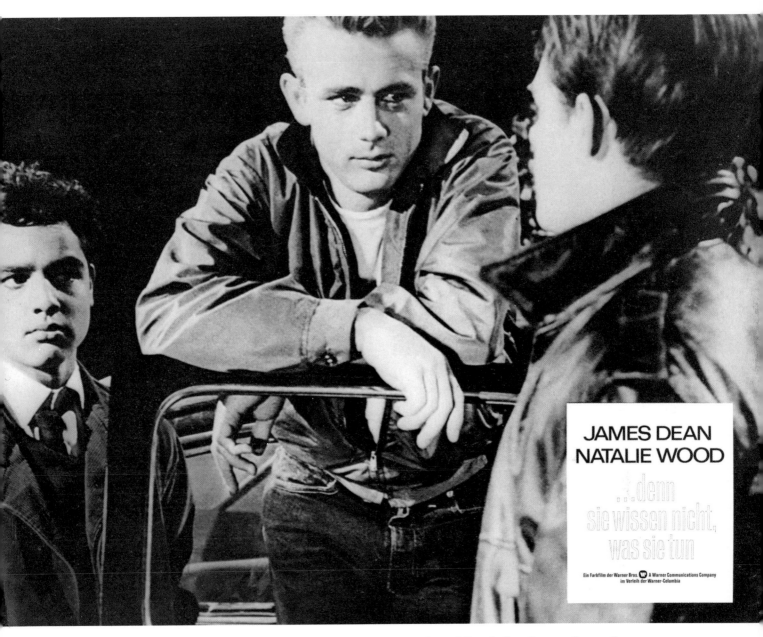

Plato (Sal Mineo) watching the psychological battle between Jim and Buzz before the test of strength.

and Jim get into their cars. They rev up their engines, and a second later we can see the two cars hurling themselves in parallel motion towards the abyss. The two drivers get ready to jump off. But Buzz has a problem: his jacket sleeve has got caught in the door. He does not want to brake because he might just be able to

81

The end of the test of strength: Goon (Dennis Hopper), Judy (Natalie Wood) and Jim (James Dean) staring down the cliff where Buzz and the car have disappeared.

jump off at the last minute if only he can somehow extricate his jacket. However, when Jim jumps off the car and lands on the ground just before he reaches the cliff, he can hear Buzz screaming as he hurtles down towards his death.

The shocked youngsters flee as fast as possible. Jim wants to give himself up to the police, but such a plan meets with his parents' disapproval, and there is a violent scene in which he and his father come to blows. Jim runs away from home and meets with his girl-friend Judy who tells him that she has also run away from her unloving father in the past. She decides that she would like to stay with Jim and never go back home again. Plato offers to help the two lovers who are not exactly Romeo and Juliet but who nevertheless find themselves in a

Jim quarrelling with Ann Doran and Jim Backus, his parents in the film.

precarious situation which might separate them for ever. He shows them his hiding-place, a deserted, empty villa where he often flees into a dream-world of his own. Without the presence of grown-ups, who always misunderstand everything anyway, Jim and Judy experience their first tender love – and also without mutual suspicion or prejudice. What is more, the three young people have at last found an opportunity to talk to one another about anything they like and to put their plans, dreams and hopes into words without outside pressure.

However, their idyllic little world is threatened by the school gang who want to take revenge on Jim because they believe that Jim has reported the

Plato, Judy and Jim in their refuge.

Jim and Judy relaxing before the highly dramatic final scene.

incident to the police. The gang approaches, and Plato suddenly produces a gun. As his parents have never taken much of an interest in him and have let him do as he wants, he simply borrowed his mother's gun shortly before going to their hide-out. Having injured one of the gang members, he fleets into the observatory where the fight between Buzz and Jim took place. By now the police have arrived. When Plato realizes what he has done, something just snaps in him. But

Jim manages to reach the observatory safely and, by talking to him patiently, to persuade him to give himself up.

But when Plato opens the heavy door of the observatory and comes into the open, he is suddenly blinded by the glaring lights of the police torches, loses his nerve and is shot by the police. By now Jim and Judy's parents have also come to the observatory and realize for the first time in their lives that they might have had their priorities wrong in

Plato on the diving-board of an empty swimming-pool, discussing philosophy with his friends. Filmed at Gloria Swanson's Villa, also the setting of "Sunset Boulevard" where William Holden plays a dead body floating in the pool.

their family lives. This, taken together with the mutual understanding which Jim and Judy have found, makes the ending an optimistic one, offering hope for a better future.

It is no mere coincidence that the hero of this film has the same first name as the actor. In a way this film reflects the problems of that particular generation, and it does so even more clearly than East of Eden. These were the problems of post-war youngsters and the generation gap and Dean had in fact experienced them himself in his own life. It is therefore hardly surprising that the background of this film is formed by Santa Monica High School – the place where, six years before, James Dean went to college shortly after moving back to California.

A whole generation of post-war youngsters shared James Dean's feelings, both in real life and in his films: they felt lonely, misunderstood and

discontented. This made Rebel Without a Cause THEIR film. Young people somehow saw themselves in this film, and they enjoyed the way in which their parents' generation had been exaggerated into caricatures.

In this film James Dean is a friend of Natalie Wood and Sal Mineo at the same time, and his role as Jim immediately made him an idol of the younger generation. People began to look upon him as the latest and most important actor since Marlon Brando. And his role finally turned him into a cultic hero of young people.

The biblical allusion in the title East of Eden was obvious. In Rebel Without a Cause, however, it comes out far more clearly in the German title: ... denn sie wissen nicht, was sie tun ("... for they do not know what they are doing"). The original English title, on the other hand, emphasizes the ambivalence of the generation conflict. Rebels without any cause for their rebellion – that was how adults viewed the younger generation.

The film shows quite accurately, though, that the youngsters of the fifties did have cause for rebellion. And not just youngsters of the fifties.

und Rennen mit gestohlenen Wagen.

Der Film zeigt uns Mitglieder dieser Welt: Den Bandenführer, das zornige verschmähte junge Mädchen, den verlorenen Aussenseiter. Vor allem erzählt er die Geschichte eines Einzelnen, die Geschichte von Jim Stark (James Dean), der sich seinen Weg bahnt. Einen Weg durch die Konfrontationen mit dem schwachen Vater, die Quälerei, in der Schule ein „Neuer" zu sein.

Die Jugendkriminalität in der Mittelschicht ist der Hintergrund dieses Films von Nicholas Ray. Im Vordergrund steht Jim Starks Weg zum Erwachsensein - in einem Tag und einer Nacht voller Leid und Zerstörung.

The film of 1955 showing James Dean as a rebel is also very popular on video cassette.

Pages 86/87: Courage is the hallmark of James Dean: In his role as Jim, he persuades the panicking Plato to give himself up to the police.

GIGANTEN
(GIANT)

EIN FARBFILM IN WARNERCOLOR

A poster for ''Giant''.

1956
Giant

A George Stevens Production.
Inspired by Edna Ferber.

Cast includes

Elizabeth Taylor	Leslie Lynton Benedict
Rock Hudson	Bick Benedict
James Dean	Jett Rink
and	
Carroll Baker	Luz Benedict II
Jane Withers	Vashti Snythe
Chill Wills	Uncle Bawley
Mercedes McCambridge	Luz Benedict
Dennis Hopper	Jordan Benedict III
Sal Mineo	Angel Obregon II
Rodney Taylor	Sir David Karfrey
Judith Evelyn	Mrs Horace Lynton
Earl Holliman	Bod Dace
Robert Nichols	Pink Snythe
Paul Fix	Dr Horace Lynton
Alexander Scourby	Old Polo
Fran Bennett	Judy Benedict
Charles Watts	Whiteside
Elsa Cardenas	Juana
Carolyn Craig	Lacey Lynton
Monte Hale	Bale Clinch
Sheb Wooley	Gabe Target
Mary Ann Edwards	Adarene Clinch
Victor Millan	Angel Obregon I
Mickey Simpson	Sarge
Pilar del Rey	Mrs Obregon
Maurice Jara	Dr Guerra
Noreen Nash	Lona Lane
Rey Whitley	Watts
Napoleon Whiting	Swazey
Screenplay	Fred Guiol and Ivan Moffat
Director of photography	William C. Mellor
Film editor	William Hornbeck
Song	"Giant" "There's never been anyone else but you" Lyrics by Paul Francis Webster Music by Dimitri Tiomkin
Musical editor	Dimitri Tiomkin
Produced by	George Stevens and Henry Ginsberg
Directed by	George Stevens

James Dean's typical gesture of helplessness: Jim holding the magazine from Plato's gun.

Filming "Rebel Without a Cause": Nicholas Ray is having a long discussion with Dean (left), as well as other actors (above: Ray, Dean, Natalie Wood). The poster (below) shows the result of this kind of work.

JAMES DEAN in "REBEL WITHOUT A CAUSE"

CINEMASCOPE and WARNERCOLOR A WARNER BROS. PICTURE WB

WARNER BROS. ZEIGEN:
EINE
GEORGE STEVENS
PRODUKTION
Giganten
GIANT
NACH DEM ROMAN VON
EDNA FERBER
ELIZABETH TAYLOR · ROCK HUDSON
JAMES D
in seiner letzte
UND
CARROL BAKER
JANE WITHERS · CHILL WILLS
EIN FARBFILM IN WARNERCOLOR
MERCEDES McCAMBRIDGE · SAL MIN
REGIE: GEORGE STEVENS

Other actors not mentioned in the credits: Felipe Turich (Gomez), Francisco Villalobos (Mexican priest), Tina Menard (Lupe), Anna Maria Majalca (Petra), Guy Teague (Harper), Natividad Vacio (Eusebio), Max Terhune (Dr Walker), Ray Bennett (Dr Borneholm), Barbara Barie (Marie Lou Decker), George Dunne (Vern Decker), Slim Talbot (Clay Hodgins), Tex Driscoll (Clay Hodgins sen.), Juney Ellis (Essie Lou Hodgins).

The film was inspired by a novel of the same name by Edna Ferber, published by Doubleday, Garden City, N.Y., in 1952 (447 pages).

Running time: 198 minutes (later versions are usually 20 minutes shorter).
Colour WarnerColor.
Filming from June to September 1955.
Première: 24 November 1956.

Summary:

After the credits our first glimpse is that of the wide expanse of the Texas landscape. A steam train is chugging across the prairie, followed by a group of cowboys on horseback. The first close-up focuses our attention on one of

the train passengers: his name is Bick Benedict (Rock Hudson), the wealthy owner of a large ranch. When he gets off the train, his importance is emphasized by the way in which the camera looks at him from below and shows a close-up of his legs and of a leather suitcase bearing his initials in large letters. James Dean does not come on the scene until considerably later. This is because he is no more than a simple farmhand before becoming a millionaire. If we were to compare Giant with that famous Texas oil epic on T.V. called Dallas, then the Benedicts could be said to correspond to the Ewings, and Jett Rink's family to the Barnes's. But as there is no trace of any J.R.-type character, we cannot push the parallel any further. Also, it is quite obvious throughout the film that it was an expensive undertaking and that it was based on a single, coherent novel, rather than a whole series of cheap weekly instalments, which is the impression that Dallas tends to give. Nor does Dallas explore the idea of the broad expanse of the Texas landscape – that giant which is always foremost in the film Giant.

Bick Benedict owns about half a million acres of land and an enormous number of cattle. One day he goes to a farm in Maryland to buy a black stallion, and on

A poster for "Giant".

Pages 96/97: George Stevens, Jr., Elizabeth Taylor, James Dean and director George Stevens inspecting one of the sites for the outside shots in Texas.

this occasion meets Leslie, a somewhat headstrong and capricious, but nevertheless charming girl. The two young people immediately fall in love with each other and get married even before Bick returns to his home ranch Reata. Life on the ranch, however, turns out to be rather an ordeal for Leslie, who has been used to the pleasantly balanced climate of Maryland. Also, people's manners are a lot more coarse, and it seems as if the scorching sun has dried up and hardened both the huge expanse of countryside and its inhabitants. Bick turns out to be stubbornly conservative and unable to take criticism from Leslie. Leslie does not approve of the way in which the Mexicans, who used to own the land, are treated like dirt and are merely kept on subsistence level.

The first decisive turning-point in the life of the Benedicts comes when Luz, Bick's elder sister, has a fatal accident with the black stallion. In her will she had decided that Jett Rink, one of the farm-hands, should be given a small plot

James Dean (with the glasses he had to wear outside his films), Rock Hudson and Elizabeth Taylor during a sumptuous feast while filming "Giant".

of land so that he can pursue his own dream of happiness. Bick is against any partioning of the Benedict property, because he regards it as an intrusion of the modern way of thinking into the nice, old-fashioned pattern of life. Jett Rink, however, rejects Bick's offer of money in exchange for the plot of land, because he is convinced that it will help him to become rich one day.

And Jett's dreams come true, though not until a few years later. By now the Benedicts have three children: a son, Jordan, and the twin sisters Judy and Luz II. And suddenly Jett hits upon that black gold called oil on his plot of land. Covered in oil from head to toe and slightly inebriated, he pays a visit to the Benedicts on their gleaming white ranch to tell them about his stroke of luck. But Bick finds Jett's behaviour rather repulsive and knocks him down with one blow. In his drunken state, however, Jett is not really capable of feeling offended. After all, he knows that the oil is going to make him a rich man, even richer than the Benedicts who have never shown any interest in oil whatsoever.

While Jett is becoming richer and more powerful every day, the Benedicts are having serious problems with their children. Jordan, who never used to enjoy playing cowboys as a child and who hated horse-riding, has decided that he wants to be a doctor and give medical

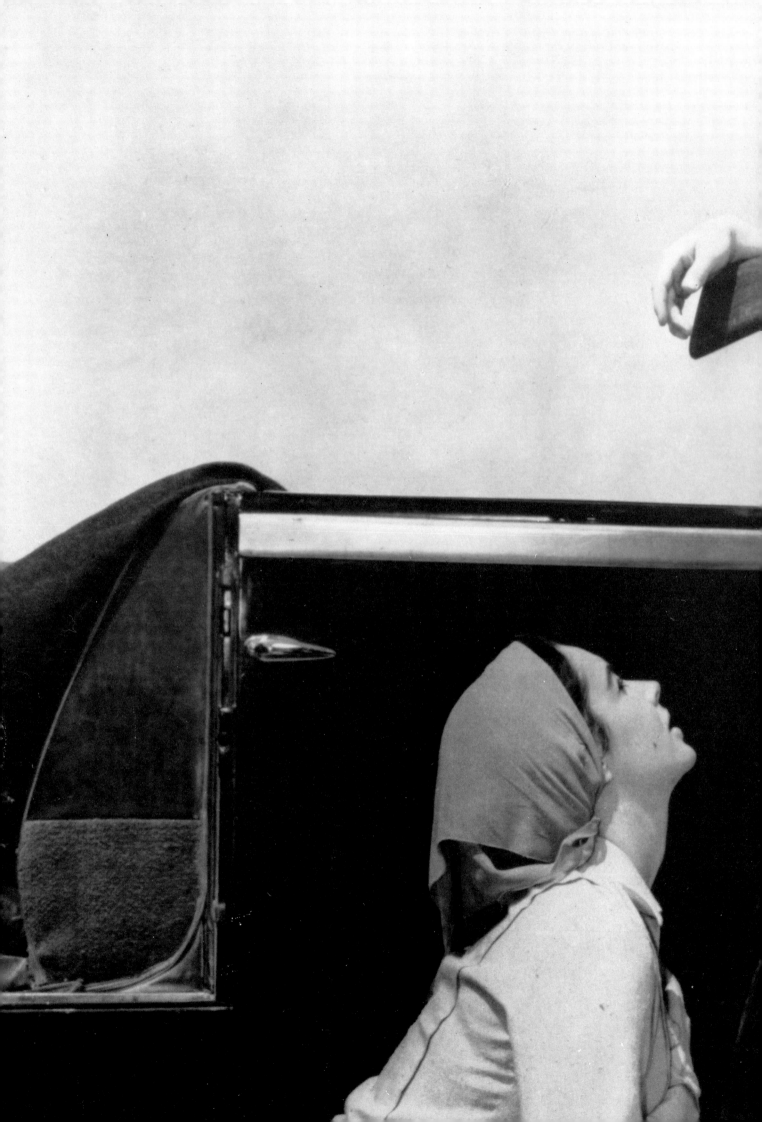

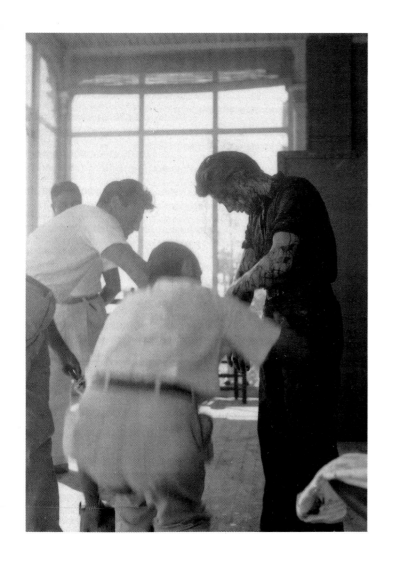

James Dean covered in oil: In for a penny, in for a pound. In the film, having found the oil well and got himself covered in it from head to toe, Jett Rink goes and sees the Benedicts. In real

Overleaf: In his role as Jett Rink in "Giant", James Dean was idolized by Leslie Benedict (Liz Taylor), just as in real life he was loved and adored by his cinema audience all over the world.

help to absolutely everyone, even the Mexicans who are despised and looked down upon by the Texans. Judy, on the other hand, refuses to be put into a ladies' finishing school in Switzerland, but would prefer to take up a career in agriculture and cattle-breeding. And

Luz II wants to remain the beautiful spoilt, rich daughter of a rancher, adored and admired by the whole world. Her idea of life does not include matrimony, because she enjoys being admired from a distance. Leslie is firmly on her children's side so that she and her husband argue and eventually separate. However, they do not stay apart for long, because Bick's love for his wife is

102

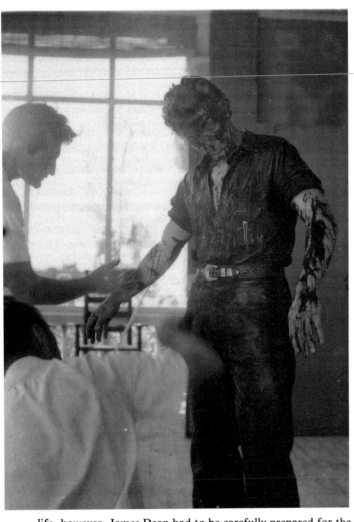
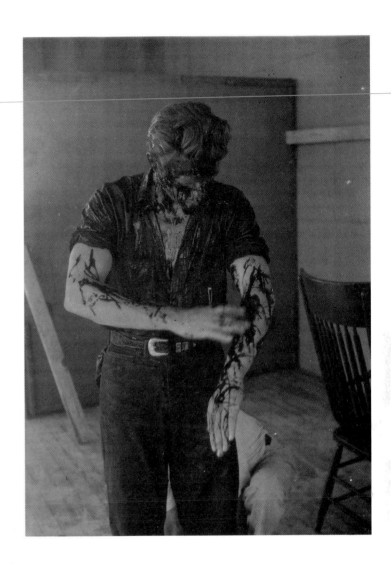

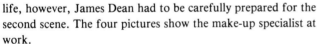

life, however, James Dean had to be carefully prepared for the second scene. The four pictures show the make-up specialist at work.

so great that he finally decides to give in to his Leslie's wishes and lets his children have their way.

At the beginning of World War II Judy gets married. Bob, her husband, does not have to join the armed forces because he is needed in the administration of the Reata Ranch. The war forces Bick Benedict to change his mind with regard to oil. The need for crude oil has by now become so enormous that Jett Rink succeeds in convincing him that it is in fact his patriotic duty to start digging for oil on his land. Very soon oil-wells are mushrooming everywhere and the great ranch house looks almost like a toy among them.

Then Jordan Benedict gets married.

Bick reluctantly has to accept the fact that his daughter-in-law is also a medical student, like his son, and that her name is Juana and she is Mexican. But there is more to come. When he goes to the opening of a four-star hotel built by Rink, he discovers his daughter Luz taking part as a Rodeo girl in the entertainment programme. Should Luz now accept Jett's proposal to marry her, that would be the last straw.

But there is enough trouble already. When Bick's Mexican daughter-in-law visits the new hotel, the staff refuse to serve her. Although Rink is still new in the class of landowners, he has taken over their outmoded values lock, stock and barrel and has decided that Mexicans should be classified as non-human and treated accordingly. Jordan rebels against these old-fashioned ideas and gets beaten up by Jett. Following old custom, Bick, the head of the family, takes this as a personal insult and challenges Jett to a fight. Jett Rink, however, is so drunk that he has already driven away all his guests and is now completely incapable of anything, let

Possessed by his own dream – this was James Dean's state of mind in "Giant" as well as in his life. Jett Rink saw the fulfilment of his dream in the form of oil.

alone a fight. Luz finds him so repulsive that she returns to the bosom of her family.

On their way to the ranch, the family decide to stop at a snack bar. When the staff there refuse to serve a group of Mexican tourists, Bick turns out to have changed considerably under the influence of his open-minded children. He protests strongly against the chauvinist contempt that is shown towards the Mexicans and gets beaten up by a group of teenagers as a result. But does this make Benedict a "failure" and Jett Rink the great winner? On the contrary, says Mrs Benedict. The Benedicts have at last been able to overcome the tyranny of their own greatness, power, and wealth – the giant who has been holding them down until now. They have become more human.

Giant has both the suspense and the epic breadth that make a tale – be it a book or a film – into an adventure. Although James Dean does not play the most important role in this film, he nevertheless provides the pivot and focal point in the life of the Benedicts and brings about a decisive change in their lives. Dean is no longer a maladjusted boy, but, like all the other actors, he has to play one person at several stages of his life. At the end of the films is 45 years old and is certainly no longer oozing charm from every pore.

Changing his age was not just a matter of clever make-up and a different posture, but Dean also had the hair above his forehead shaved off, to indicate a receding hairline. When Dean died in a car accident near Paso Robles two days after the completion of the film, he was only 24 but had the appearance of a man in his forties.

Not only were the screen characters first class "giants", but also the actors themselves: apart from James Dean, above all Elizabeth Taylor and Rock Hudson, who injected a breath of life into Edna Ferber's novel about the beginning of the oil age. The critics realized that Dean was capable of acting more than the confused teenager. But their change of mind came too late for Dean. Rock Hudson made his way to the top with this film. Elizabeth Taylor had already been a film star for some time, but her dramatic expertise did not really become fully obvious until later, when she played together with Richard Burton. Although she was of course excellent in this film, she did not manage to age quite as superbly as her colleagues. Another giant we must not ignore was undoubtedly George Stevens, the film director. And of course there was Dimitri Tiomkin who provided the sort of musical background that was more than adequate. The result of this gigantic team effort was a film which can be rightly called a "James Dean film", even though Dean did not have the most important role. But it was also a film that turned out to be one of the greatest money-spinners which Warner Brothers produced in the 1950s. Their studios made a profit of 12 million dollars, which was a tremendous amount of money at the time.

Luz II (Carroll Baker) is being visited by Jett Rink, now a smart, middle-aged gentleman.

Pages 108/109: Having made his fortune, Jett Rink finally ends up as a failure and turns to alcohol for comfort. James Dean was still wearing the outward signs of his age in the film when he had his fatal car accident.

The James Dean Cult
or
The Everlasting Youth of the Fifties

In his native America James Dean gained recognition as an actor only gradually and when he became a Hollywood film star he had already been acting in television programmes for quite some time. The rest of the world, on the other hand, was completely taken by surprise. All of a sudden people were faced with a young man who, in colour and CinemaScope, embodied all the fears and anxieties of the post-war generation and who successfully gave expression to these fears in his films. His postures and mannerisms as well as his unquenchable desire for love made a deep impression on his public. His attitude was that of a certain weariness of life, a romantic discontent, a deep sadness at the world's woes, continuing the poetic tradition of Byron and the philosophical one of Schopenhauer. This outlook of his struck the right chord with his contemporaries who were torn by the generation conflict and full of anxieties about the atom bomb.

Suddenly everyone wanted to be like James Dean: people began to imitate his style of clothes, his nonchalance, his refusal to give in. He was giving them new values at a time when old values were felt to be crumbling. People had an example again, something to cling to and to love and cherish with all their heart. This is one reason why we can speak of a James Dean cult, especially – but not just – after his death. Gradually however, this naive pseudo-cult began to make room for a more sober approach, when people began to see Dean and his idolization more as a phenomenon of his time.

Surprisingly, however, although Dean was the personification of a particular age, he managed to outlive that age. Dean can speak to us even today. Also, it is an important feature of the eighties that, side by side with all the progress, there is an element of nostalgia: people are increasingly paying attention to the age of kidney-shaped tables and the beginnings of rock-'n-roll. Dean has become a historical figure, which makes him re-usable and valid as a pop icon. Although it is probably mere coincidence, it is nevertheless interesting to note that Andy Warhol made use of Campbell soups for his pop art, i.e. the same company which sponsored and promoted the television plays that paved James Dean's road to success.

There has, of course, been a certain amount of controversy about Dean's fame. To commemorate the 30th

This picture from "Giant" is probably the best-known one of James Dean.

JAMES DEAN
ELIZABETH TAYLOR
ROCK HUDSON

Giganten

Ein Farbfilm der Warner Bros.
A Warner Communications Company
im Verleih der Warner-Columbia

anniversary of his death, the German magazin <u>Der Spiegel</u> asked their readers if they thought of James Dean as the first male sex symbol, a kind of public human pet. Although many readers wrote back indignantly, there were also quite a few who whole-heartedly agreed with the magazine's attempt to topple the idol. Nevertheless James Dean has been and still is a memorial to himself, a living myth. And the more people read into James Dean, or the more they criticize him, the more legendary he becomes. As with any other legend or cult, it is fed not only by the enthusiasm of his admirers, but also by the criticism of his scoffers. When driven into a corner – even if it is only for the purpose of making someone think – people tend to cling to their convictions even more strongly than before.

Nowadays it is perhaps not so much Dean's rebelliousness which people identify with, but rather his inner strife, his feeling of being torn, not knowing where he belongs or what to do with one's life. Television producers and editors of teenage magazines are well aware of this, and so are advertisers. The topic 'James Dean' has not sunk

Der Tag an dem James Dean starb

Das steht nur in BRAVO

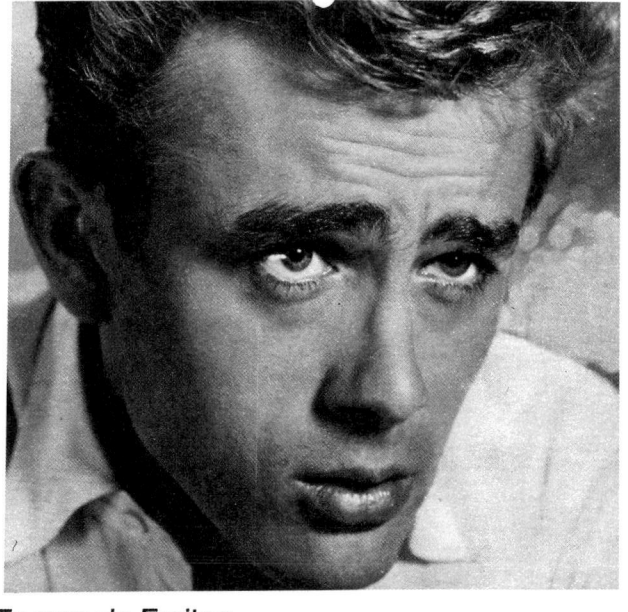

Es war ein Freitag.
Freitag, der 30. September 1955. An diesem Tag endete sein strahlendes junges Leben in den Trümmern seines silbergrauen Sportwagens. Aber für alle, die ihn liebten, ist er nie gestorben! Darum schreibt jetzt BRAVO die große Geschichte des unvergessenen, unvergeßlichen JAMES DEAN! Die ganze Wahrheit!

When James Dean became famous he changed into a magic popular icon, as in this water-colour which is reminiscent of his hungry days in New York: "Boulevard of Broken Dreams" by Gottfried Helnwein, 1981, 210 x 150 cms (after a photograph by Denis Stock). Copyright Gottfried Helnwein.

The tenth anniversary of James Dean's death was commemorated specially by the German teenage magazine Bravo. To attract readers, special advertisements were printed in the most popular German equivalents of the Radio and T.V. Times: "The day James Dean died. It was a Friday. Friday the 30th September 1955. This was the day when his blooming young life ended in the wreckage of his silver grey sports car. But for all those who loved him he never died! And so BRAVO is now writing the great story of the unforgotten, unforgettable JAMES DEAN! The whole truth!"

The well-known picture form "Giant" had been identified so much with James Dean that it was used for a completely different film in France, i.e. for "East of Eden".

In "Badlands" (1974) Martin Sheen played a young killer who took James Dean as his example in 1959. Film magazines showed the obvious parallels in their photographs.

into oblivion yet, ans so there is still a great danger of misinterpretation and misunderstandings. In 1986, for example, a jeans firm launched an advertising campaign in which they tried to re-create the Dean atmosphere of the fifties. What they did not realize, however, was that in Giant Dean was wearing a pair of jeans that had been manufactured by a different firm and that this was quite obvious to anyone who knew anything about jeans.

But quite apart form the whole area of commerce and advertising: What does James Dean today mean to the generation of people who had first-hand experience of him? Does he still represent the eternal youth of the fifties for them? I think he does. And there is indeed some indication that this is the case. Helmut Dietl's television programmes on German T.V., such as Münchner Geschichten, prove conclusively that James Dean is alive. It would probably be an exaggeration to describe the German actor Wolfgang Fierek as an exact imitation of James Dean, but it is nevertheless true that he follows in his footsteps. In the seventies, in the film Badlands, Martin Sheen was deliberately cast in the mould of James Dean. One can give an endless list of examples where, to a greater or lesser extent, James Dean has been influential and still is.

But there is another aspect in which James Dean is still significant today. That generation in which Dean grew up and which is now the older generation has found a never-ceasing rejuvenating force in the unaging film image of their former idol. Dean's films conjure up the same atmosphere and the same feelings which they had when they first watched them thirty years ago. On the one hand, this leads to a certain wistfulness when

Within the image:

Mit 20 kann man noch auf 10 qm glücklich sein.

Irgendwann ist es soweit: die erste sturmfreie Bude. Weil aber bald die Ansprüche steigen, sollten Sie rechtzeitig vorbauen.

Am besten gleich mit einem Bausparvertrag von Wüstenrot. Damit beginnen Sie heute schon Ihr Wohneigentum von morgen zu sichern. Und das auch dann, wenn Sie noch nicht viel verdienen. Denn Bausparen wird vom Staat nach wie vor mit hohen Prämien belohnt.

Fragen Sie Ihren Wüstenrot-Berater. Er weiß Bescheid.

Das Glück braucht ein Zuhause- bauen wir's auf.

wüstenrot

Wüstenrot, a German building society, tried to attract young savers in an advertisement in Der Spiegel in 1981: Note the James Dean poster in the corner of the picture.

they realize that they are getting older and older compared with James Dean. On the other hand, however, these films also awaken reminiscences of the generation gap of their time and might make people a little more sensitive towards the one that exists today.

Obviously James Dean cannot have the same rejuvenating function for present-day youngsters that he has for their parents' generation. However, he is still a tangible reality for them. Although there are innumerable new and similar idols today, and James Dean is only one among many others, there are signs that he has reached a certain timelessness which many of today's idols do not have or do not want to have. He comes from a pre-throwaway era and has left an indelible impression on people's minds that might outlast the age of plastic.

In December 1956, shortly before "Giant" was shown in German cinemas, Bravo launched its own powerful advertising campaign, thus initiating the German version of the James Dean cult.

BRAVO

Die Zeitschrift für Film und Fer

Nr. 15

2. Dezember 1956 · 50 Pfennig

Postverlagsort München

Liz Taylor, eine der wenigen,
die weiß, woran James Dean
wirklich zerbrach

n Gigant unter

GIGANTEN:

ames Dean
n seinem
etzten Film

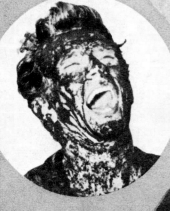

Sonderbericht aus Hollywood:
Ich war Jimmys Freund

BRAVO

Die Zeit... ...it dem jungen Herzen

Nr. 15 · 14. April 195... · Fernsehen · Schlager · 50 Pf. · Postverlagsort München

Seine Freunde sind sich einig:
Das ist eines der schönsten,
charakteristischsten James-
Dean-Fotos. Das ist Jimmy!

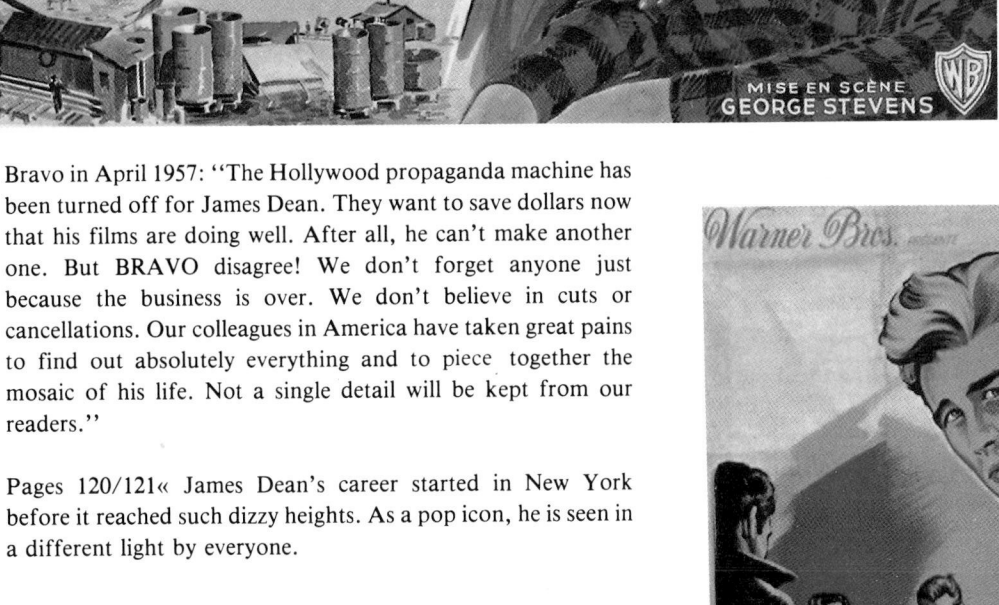

Dean posters are popular all over the world and are often reprinted on postcards.

Bravo in April 1957: "The Hollywood propaganda machine has been turned off for James Dean. They want to save dollars now that his films are doing well. After all, he can't make another one. But BRAVO disagree! We don't forget anyone just because the business is over. We don't believe in cuts or cancellations. Our colleagues in America have taken great pains to find out absolutely everything and to piece together the mosaic of his life. Not a single detail will be kept from our readers."

Pages 120/121« James Dean's career started in New York before it reached such dizzy heights. As a pop icon, he is seen in a different light by everyone.

The question is sometimes asked whether James Dean's fame would have lasted if he had not died in 1955 and how he might have developed as a person and as an actor. But such a question, legimate though it may be, is purely speculative. It could perhaps serve as a good starting point for a film or a novel, but the result of such idle speculation could not change the facts. James Dean would remain what he always has been: a memorial to himself – a memorial about which everybody has his own ideas.

Films and Television Programmes about James Dean

The media soon realized that James Dean's arrival was a stroke of luck for them and that he could continue to serve their purposes even after his death. Warner Brothers, who had originally planned more films with James Dean, produced the first documentary about his life and his dramatic achievements. It appeared in 1956, was 82 minutes long and was called The James Dean Story, written by Stewart Stern, produced by George W. George and directed by Robert Altman. The most striking thing about this black-and-white film, which was first shown in October 1957, was the advertisement which announced: "James Dean plays himself in The James Dean Story."

In an NBC television show on 14 October 1956 Steve Allen presented the first detailed programme about James Dean's life.

This was followed by a CBS television documentary in 1957, called A Tribute to James Dean.

In February 1974 the ABC began to take an interest in the subject and broadcast a programme called James Dean: Memories of a Gentle Giant. Several interviews with Dean's former frineds and colleagues were also included.

Then there was the ABC series Dick Clark Presents the Rock and Roll Years, from November 1973 to January 1974, where James Dean was also talked about in detail.

Another film that was made in 1974 was the British colour documentary James Dean: The First American Teenager. This 80-minute film reached the cinemas in 1975. It has been shown on German and Austrian television several times since 1977, and there are a number of odd inaccuracies in the German version. One of Dean's contemporaries, for example, talks about the things they used to do at Googie's Restaurant, and she is promptly corrected by the German commentator who somehow seemed to prefer an Italianized form: Gucci's Restaurant. Germans may of course wonder whether the G is hard or soft, i.e. whether it should be Goodgie or Googhie, but a television commentator of today ought to assume that an American of the fifties knows better how to pronounce a particular name of that period.

In 1977 there was even a musical called Dean. It was shown at the London

A German souvenir brochure for "Giant" with the appropriate title: "James Dean – a short life for the film."

JAMES DEAN

Ein kurzes Leben für den Film

Casino Theatre, with Glenn Conway playing the film star. However, it was taken off after only one week, and the design of the film poster eventually turned out to be of a more lasting quality than the musical itself.

1977 also saw the production of the film 9/30/55. The script was by James Bridges, who also acted produced the film. The title is the date of Dean's death, i.e. September 30th, 1955. The film is about the death of a young idol called Jimmy J. and its effect on his adolescent admirers. Jimmy is played by Richard Thomas, known as John Boy in The Waltons.

In 1981 the Bliss Theatre in Munich gave their interpretation of the Dean myth. From 7 February onwards, every Saturday and Sunday night, Hanni Stadler and Günther Geiermann recited a text collage called Der Tod des James Dean ('The Death of James Dean'), which had been put together by Alfred Andersch.

A four-part television series about James Dean would be bound to attract people and could include his three films and one of the two films about him.

Pages 124/125: James Dean at the cinema. A highly significant scene from "The James Dean Story".

Appendix

James Dean on Record

Warner Bros. Records 3XX2737
50 YEARS OF FILM
This album commemorates the 50th anniversary of Warner Brothers. It includes a glossy brochure and three LPs with particularly important extracts of varying lengths from their films. The third LP (side 5) includes extracts from James Dean's films. In East of Eden (1955) he is shown in a scene with Raymond Massey and Richard Davalos, in Rebel Without a Cause (1955) with his film parents Ann Davalos and Jim Backus, and in Giant (1956) with Rock Hudson, Elizabeth Taylor and Chill Wills.

Bibliography

Bast, William, James Dean. A Biography. New York 1956

Bosworth, Patricia, Montgomery Clift. New York 1978

Dalton, David, James Dean – The Mutant King. 1974

Dimmitt, Richard Bertrand, A Title Guide to the Talkies, New York, London 1965

Hirschhorn, Clive, The Warner Bros. Story. London 1983

Howlett, John, James Dean, London 1975

Kael, Pauline, I Lost It at the Movies. Boston, 1965

Maltin, Leonard, Movie Comedy Teams. New York 1970

Marcks, Michael, James Dean. Rebell and Idol. (Von Fans für Fans Nr. 2). Celle/West Germany 1978

Martinetti, Ronald, The James Dean Story. New York 1975

Morella, Joe and Edward Z. Epstein, Rebels. The Rebel Hero in Films. Secaucus, N.J. 1973

Roth, Sanford and Beulah Roth, James Dean. Munich/West Germany 1984

Silke, James R., Here's Looking at You, Kid. Boston/Toronto 1976

Steinbeck, John, East of Eden. Viking Press Inc. 1952

Stuart, Ray, Immortals of the Screen. New York 1965

Terrace, Vincent, Encyclopedia of Television Series, Pilots and Specials 1937 – 1973. New York 1986

Wilk, Max, The Golden Age of Television. New York 1976

Worth, Fred L., The Complete Unabridged Super Trivia Encyclopedia. New York 1977.

Zinman, David, 50 from the 50s, New Rochelle, New York 1979.

Acknowledgements:

The author and producers of this book are grateful to all those picture agencies and photographic archives listed below for permission to reproduce the pictures and photographs used in this book. Our special thanks to Warner Bros. who sponsored James Dean and enabled him to become famous. We also thank Gottfried Helnwein for his portrait of James Dean.

The photographs of James Dean and of his films produced by Warner Bros. have been taken from the following archives:

The John Kobal Collection:
6, 8/9, 13, 14/15, 18, 19, 20/21, 23, 24, 26/27, 28, 29, 31, 32, 34, 35, 40, 42, 50/51, 58, 59, 74, 76/77, 83 below, 84, 85, 92, 93 above, 93 below, 98, 100 left, 100/101, 102 left, 102 right, 103 left, 103 right, 104, 108/109.

Filmarchiv Lothar Just:
10, 46/47, 49, 56 above, 60/61, 68/69, 78/79, 80, 81, 82, 91, 96/97, 107, 111, 123, 124/125.

Filmarchiv Robert Fischer:
36/37, 55, 56 below, 62, 63, 64/65, 67, 73, 83 above, 86/87, 94, 119 above, 119 below.

Advertisements, magazines and film posters are from the author's own archives.

The water-colour painting on p. 112 has been reproduced with the kind permission of Gottfried Helnwein.